DIGITAL CITIZENS

MY
DIGITAL
FUTURE

BEN HUBBARD

ILLUSTRATED BY DIEGO VAISBERG

Lerner Publications ◆ Minneapolis

First American edition published in 2019 by Lerner
Publishing Group, Inc.

First published in Great Britain in 2018 by
The Watts Publishing Group
Copyright © The Watts Publishing
Group 2018

Credits
Series Editor: Julia Bird
Illustrator: Diego Vaisberg
Packaged by: Collaborate

Lerner Publications Company
A division of Lerner Publishing Group, Inc.
241 First Avenue North
Minneapolis, MN 55401 USA

For reading levels and more information, look up
this title at www.lernerbooks.com.

Main body text set in Courier PS Std.
Typeface provided by Monotype Typography.

Library of Congress Cataloging-in-Publication Data

Names: Hubbard, Ben, 1973- author. | Vaisberg, Diego, illustrator.
Title: My digital future / Ben Hubbard ; [illustrated by] Diego
Vaisberg.
Description: Minneapolis : Lerner Publications, [2019] | Series:
Digital citizens | Includes bibliographical references and index.
Identifiers: LCCN 2018028520 (print) | LCCN 2018029302 (ebook) | ISBN
9781541543065 (eb pdf) | ISBN 9781541538795 (lb : alk. paper)
Subjects: LCSH: Information technology—Social aspects—Juvenile
literature. | Internet and children—Juvenile literature.
Classification: LCC HM851 (ebook) | LCC HM851 H837 2019 (print) | DDC
303.48/33—dc23

LC record available at https://lccn.loc.gov/2018028520

Manufactured in the United States of America
1-45062-35889-8/6/2018

CONTENTS

WHAT IS DIGITAL CITIZENSHIP?

When we log onto the internet, we become part of a giant online world.

In this world we can use our smartphones, tablets, and computers to explore, create, and communicate with billions of different people. Together, these people make up a global digital community. That is why they are known as digital citizens. When you use the internet you are a digital citizen too. So what does this mean?

CITIZEN VS DIGITAL CITIZEN

A good citizen is someone who behaves well, looks after themselves and others, and tries to make their community a better place. A good digital citizen acts exactly the same way. However, the online world is bigger than just a local neighborhood, city, or country. It spans the whole world and crosses every kind of border. It is therefore up to all digital citizens everywhere to make this digital community a safe, fun, and exciting place for everyone.

MY DIGITAL FUTURE

Digital technology is how we manage our lives in the modern world. Many people stay logged in to the internet, their networks, and the wider online community using mobile and wearable devices. Keeping up to date with trends in digital technology is an important part of being a digital citizen. The future, after all, will be digital. But what developments might this bring? This book explores the world of digital technology today and how it might look tomorrow.

FUTURE TECHNOLOGY TODAY

In the modern world, we are surrounded by digital technology.

There are smartphones, tablets, and wearable devices wherever we go. Our homes contain computers, gaming consoles, and smart appliances. The internet is what connects all of these devices and the people who use them. In the future, however, it will make us more connected than ever before.

SMART FAMILIES

Today, families often communicate by sending instant messages and emails or checking social media posts. Sometimes they do this even while they are in the same home! Some homes, however, have taken their digital technology to the next level with "smart" appliances that are connected to the internet. This means lights, ovens, and security systems can control themselves or be managed remotely from a smartphone. Sometimes, these appliances are linked to a central "hub" robot that can walk around, talk, and recognize household members.

THE INTERNET OF THINGS

Smart appliances in the home are part of the Internet of Things (IoT). This refers to connected devices that talk to each other and us over the internet. An example is a smart fridge that messages us when it is running out of milk. However, in the future the IoT is predicted to operate on a much bigger scale than just home appliances. This could mean fitness collars that would tell us when to exercise our dogs, garbage cans that message us when they are full, and traffic lights that interact with our self-driving cars to ensure no one gets caught in traffic.

DATING DIGITAL DEVICES

The rate of technology is moving so fast that new digital devices seem to go out of date almost as soon as they are unveiled.

However, staying informed about new technologies is an important part of being a digital citizen. So what digital trends are predicted for the near future?

ROBOTS ABOUT

Robots have been all around us now for many years. There are robots working in factories, hospitals, and homes at this very moment. There have been robot pets for decades, and it may not be long before we see robot assistants in shops and restaurants.

MORE REALITY

Virtual Reality (VR) headsets were often first used in gaming. They allowed users to see and interact in virtual 3D worlds like they were actually there. However, VR headsets can now also be used to browse, buy, and use apps; design aircraft and cars; and explore simulated environments on Earth. It is predicted VR will soon be used to interact with live environments and other people— all from the comfort of your home. This could mean having front row seats at a sports game, attending school lessons, or visiting your doctor, all by simply putting on a VR headset.

EXCUSE ME, MISS, WHAT IS A "SMARTPHONE"?

WEAR IT WELL

Wearable digital technology allows us to access the internet from devices such as smart watches or glasses, avoiding the need for a digital device that we carry around. Controlling our devices by voice is also a new way of cutting back on screen use. It is predicted that smart glasses or headsets controlled by our voices could soon beam images directly into our eyes. This could one day make smartphones a gadget of the past.

DRONE DELIVERIES

In 2016, the first pizzas were delivered by drone. Now, new drones are being developed that deliver people! These drones are being designed to pick people up and fly them to work or school without them having to steer. Maybe the future for young digital citizens will include attending school lessons by using a VR headset while being taken from place to place by personal drone!

THE LATEST THING

As consumers of new technology, digital citizens are often urged to "buy, buy, buy." Technology companies constantly compete to release the latest gadget, and their advertisements insist we cannot live without it. An important part of being a digital citizen is understanding how to use today's technology. But how can we stay digitally literate without being pressured to purchase the "latest thing"?

DON'T BELIEVE THE HYPE

Clever digital citizens know how to keep up to date with new technology without having to actually buy it. This is easily achieved by doing some research online. Reading online technology magazines and watching reviews of new gadgets is a great first step. This can keep you in the loop without having to spend money.

GREATEST, NOT LATEST

It's easy to see a new gadget advertised and fool ourselves into believing we can't live without it. However, with time this passes. After all, does your current gadget still work? Then why replace it? It's also important to realize the latest thing is not always the greatest thing. It's best to ignore our impulses to buy things and instead carefully evaluate what we need and what we don't. This is how clever digital citizens avoid being sucked into a never-ending buying loop.

DIGITAL MAINTENANCE

Have you ever lost or broken your smartphone or tablet? It can be a bitter blow.

Sometimes it's only when these devices are gone that we realize how much we use them. That's why smart digital citizens take care of their digital devices and keep them in good working order. These tips can show you how.

WHAT'S THAT YOU'VE GOT?

THIS IS A STEEL-REINFORCED, LEAD-LINED PROTECTION BOX FOR MY PHONE. IT SHOULD NOW BE ABLE TO SURVIVE A NUCLEAR BLAST.

CASE PROTECTED

Buying a case and a screen protector for your digital device is a good, simple form of protection. These will keep your devices from becoming scratched and may save them from breaking if they are dropped.

SAFE STORAGE

Have a safe spot where you keep your digital device when it is not in use, such as a bookshelf. Keep your charger there too. This will keep your device from being sat or stepped on and also can help prevent you misplacing it.

PRESERVE YOUR BATTERY

Cell phone batteries can last years if properly taken care of. The best way of doing this is to charge them regularly. Experts say keeping your phone battery at between 40 percent and 80 percent will greatly increase its life. A simpler tip is to try not to let your phone's battery drop below a 40 percent charge.

DRY, NOT WET

It may seem obvious, but don't get your device wet by using it in the rain. Also be extra careful around open water, such as rivers, the sea, and toilets!

IN SIGHT, OUT OF MIND

Never let your device out of sight when in public. Also make sure you have set a passcode on your device in case it ever gets stolen. This will prevent a thief from accessing your information. You can even download anti-theft software to shut down and locate your phone if it is stolen. Ask your trusted adult for help with this.

UPDATE SOFTWARE

Carrying out software updates on your digital device can stop it from being infected by viruses or malware. This is because software updates are often released soon after new harmful bugs and viruses have been detected. Software updates almost always improve your phone's performance too.

13

EXPLAINING THE WORLD

Blogs, instructional videos, and video blogs (vlogs) are an excellent way to learn from the experts online.

These can give us information about how things work or hands-on advice on building things. They can also provide us with tutorials of online games and reviews of the latest technology. They can help us become both capable digital citizens and informed consumers.

HOW TO DO IT...

Have you ever dreamed about making a smartphone projector? Or perhaps a simple robot? It's easy to learn how with instructional videos. Simply type what you'd like to make into a video-sharing website or a general search engine.

USEFUL REVIEWS

Part of being a smart digital citizen is staying informed about the latest digital technology and what it promises to do. It's easy to find reviews on a new product by entering its name and "review" into a search engine. Reviews often show that the latest thing isn't what it's cracked up to be, which can save you a lot of money and heartache.

GAME TUTORIALS

All gamers know the frustration of being defeated at a
difficult point in a game—over and over and over again.
Tutorials of video games can help immensely with these tricky
bits. They can also offer cheats if you've really had enough
of doing it the honest way. Simply drop your game's name and
"tutorial" or "cheat" into a search engine.

"It's too
expensive,
it doesn't
have a
headphone jack,
and it is no better
than the previous
model.Avoid!"

ONLINE SHOPPING

Shopping online is so popular that many people use it for almost all of their purchases.

It is possible to buy virtually anything online, but shopping this way can present some risks. Fake websites are a common danger. However, clever digital citizens know how to spot a fake website so they won't get scammed.

THIS ONE'S SUPER CHEAP.

PERHAPS IT'S TOO GOOD TO BE TRUE. DID YOU LOOK AT THE "SPOT THE FAKE WEBSITE" CHECKLIST?

SPOT THE FAKE WEBSITE

You've found a website that offers the same products as elsewhere but for much lower prices. Sound too good to be true? It probably is. Investigate the website by following this checklist:

1 Does it have broken English, spelling mistakes, or odd-sounding text?

2 Has the website's domain name been recently registered? Your trusted adult can help you look this up.

16

SPOT THE FAKE REVIEW

Sometimes fake websites post fake reviews to convince people that they are genuine. If there are a number of reviews that have been recently posted, this can be a sign that the reviews are fake. If the reviews are short, do not give much information, and are all worded in the same way, this can be another tell-tale sign. If you find any such reviews about a website, it is probably best to steer clear of it altogether.

MOM, YOU WERE RIGHT. THIS WEBSITE LOOKS FAKE.

3 Does the website have any contact details, such as a phone number, street address, or email address?

4 Is there a "returns" page with a clear returns policy?

5 Has anyone had trouble with the website before? Check this out by dropping the website's name and the word "review" into a search engine. If the answers to any of these questions are "yes," avoid it!

TECHNOLOGY IN BUSINESS

Digital technology has been of great benefit to businesses.

Twenty years ago, an office worker making a video conference call via their smartphone would have been unthinkable. Today it is commonplace. Now, young digital entrepreneurs are making a name for themselves by creating new social media platforms, apps, and games. Others are using digital technology to address environmental issues affecting our planet.

FOR THE GREATER GOOD

Although many digital entrepreneurs have made millions, not all are motivated by money. Many want to use digital technology to help people and save the planet. Some do this by using the internet to raise awareness for the work they do. Others invent new technologies to help people in need. Some examples of these follow.

GREEN APPS

There are green apps available that help people become more environmentally minded. These include apps that scan barcodes to tell you where a product comes from and if its manufacturer harms the environment. Another records your carbon footprint and suggests ways of cutting it down.

ONLINE ENTREPRENEURS

Entrepreneurs have looked for ways of making money from the internet since it was launched. Social media platforms have made many people extremely rich, as have apps and online games. Some of those behind new social media platforms, apps, and games are only in their teens.

BIO-FUEL COULD POWER MANY OF THE WORLD'S VEHICLES INSTEAD OF POLLUTING GASOLINE.

SMART SAVINGS

Smart homes run by a central computer or robot connected to the internet aim to eliminate energy waste in the home. They do this by switching off lights when nobody is in the room, using appliances at night when energy is cheaper, and powering down any appliance that is not in active use.

SPREAD THE WORD

Video websites that feature inspiring speakers are easy to find on the internet. Some of these sites have an emphasis on tackling environmental issues and keeping the world green. Such video sites raise awareness, help people collaborate, and make us think about the issues facing the world.

TECHNOLOGY IN SCHOOLS

Schools around the world use digital technology differently.

Some schools have no digital technology at all. Others have strict rules about how it can be used. The best schools are those that use digital technology to develop collaborative projects with students. These projects can help spread the word about being a good digital citizen.

SOCIALLY RESPONSIBLE

Social media sites sometimes receive negative press because they can be used by students to bully others. But they can also be used to spread anti-bullying messages. The students of one school used social media to discuss why bullying is wrong and also define what it means to be a good digital citizen. The group described a good digital citizen as: "An individual who is aware, empathetic, and socially responsible, both face to face and online." The students then shared their findings via video conferencing with different schools and a panel of adult education experts.

MEET YOUR STUDENTS

A group of digital educators have created a social media website that shares the views of both teachers and students. Articles and vlogs about being digital citizens can then be viewed by others. This helps students feel their opinions are valued too.

EDUCATING THE WORLD

Clever digital citizens want to live in a world of online users who can use technology well.

This means helping other people to use their digital devices. Many older people were not surrounded by online technology when they were growing up. This means they can sometimes need younger people to help them.

LET ME SHOW YOU HOW TO USE IT, DAD.

BE A GOOD DIGITAL TEACHER

The followings tips can help you become a good digital teacher, even with adults that can't use their digital devices properly!

DON'T ASSUME

Some people have never heard of social media or mobile apps! If you're showing someone how to do something online, don't assume they will understand what any of the names mean.

GETTING THE BASICS

If you're showing someone how to do something online, just teach them the basics first. Otherwise it's easy for them to get overwhelmed. Once they've got it, you can show them more.

PRAISE IS GOOD

Even adults need to be told that they are doing a good job sometimes! Saying things like "That's good" and "You've got it" can make a big difference.

BE PATIENT

Everyone learns in different ways, so it's important not to get irritated if someone doesn't understand something right away.

KEEP LEARNING

There's always more to learn about online technology, and smart digital citizens make sure they are up to date with what's new. Never feel afraid to ask someone about new technology.

TECHNOLOGY TOMORROW

Many people worry that technology is ruling our lives.

They say the digital devices that were created as tools now control us. How much we should allow new technology into our lives is a question all digital citizens should consider. This will help form our ideas about future technology.

BECOMING CYBORGS

After we tire of smartphones and wearable technology, experts predict that people will turn to digital implants. This could include having a surgically-added device that connects your brain directly to the internet. Another eye implant would enable you to bring up a screen in front of you whenever you like. For many this is too much like creating cyborgs—humans that are mixed with machines. What do you think?

CAN YOU SWITCH OFF?

Digital citizens can sometimes struggle to turn off their devices. However, the internet is going to become more of a feature in our lives, not less. How much you use this technology is for you to decide. Ask yourself: "Is it harming my body or my mind?" or "Is it preventing me from doing other things I enjoy offline?" Most of all: "Is it making me feel good?" If you are unsure why you are even spending time online, maybe it's time to turn off your digital devices and take a break.

THANKS. BUT HOW DID YOU SEND THEM?

I CONNECTED WITH MY WI-FI IMPLANT, LOOKED UP YOUR NUMBER ON MY EYEBALL SCREEN, AND WROTE A MESSAGE USING MY BRAIN WAVES. IT'S ALL THOUGHT-CONTROLLED IN THE FUTURE!

THE FUTURE IS UNWRITTEN

Nobody knows for sure what will come next in our digital world.

That is why it is important for digital citizens to discuss what being a good digital citizen means. Most agree that good digital citizens have certain qualities. These include trustworthiness, kindness, and empathy. But what are the other qualities? What do you think? After all, the digital future is a blank page ready to be written by citizens like you.

DIGITAL CITIZENS TO DIGITAL CREATORS

Perhaps it seems strange to list the qualities that digital citizens should have, but that's because young digital citizens of today like you will be the digital creators of tomorrow. This means you'll be deciding what kind of place the online world will be and how digital citizens should behave within it. With your help, the online world will be a safe, fun, and exciting place for all!

Good digital citizens should:

1 Respect themselves and other people online.

2 Protect themselves and the personal information of people around them.

3 Believe in free speech, as long as it doesn't hurt others.

4 Respect the laws and digital rules of their parents and school.

5 Show kindness and compassion to other digital citizens.

6 Believe everyone should have access to the internet.

7 Look after their physical and mental well-being while they are online.

DIGITAL QUIZ

Now that you've reached the end of this book, how do you feel about your digital future?

How much have you learned? And how much can you remember? Take this quiz and tally up your score at the end to find out.

1. What does IoT stand for?
a. Internet on Top
b. Internet of Things
c. Internet or Thing

2. What were Virtual Reality headsets originally often used for?
a. Gaming
b. Jogging
c. Seeing into the future

3. Why should you carry out software updates on your smartphone?
a. It could win you a new phone
b. It can prevent it from being infected by the latest virus
c. Otherwise it could catch fire

4. If an online website does not have a contacts page or returns policy you should . . .
a. Not buy anything from it
b. Only purchase small items from it
c. Email the administrator to ask if the site is genuine

5. What quality is important to show when teaching others?
a. Irritation
b. Confusion
c. Patience

6. What is a common way digital entrepreneurs have become rich from the internet?
a. Apps
b. Wraps
c. Taps

7. What should you do with your digital device in public?

a. Show it off
b. Ask strangers to hold it
c. Never let it out of your sight

8. What might replace smartphones in the future?

a. Digital implants
b. Tin cans
c. Robots that we can talk into

HOW DID YOU DO? ADD UP YOUR SCORE TO SEE.

1-4: You are on your way, but retake the quiz to get a score over 4.

5-7: You've passed the quiz well. Now see if you can pass the quiz in the book *My Digital Community and Media*.

8: Wow! 8 out of 8. You are a natural born digital citizen!

ANSWERS

1: b; 2: a; 3: b; 4: a; 5: c; 6: c; 7: a; 8: a

GLOSSARY

apps
Short for "applications,"
apps are computer program for
mobile digital devices, such as
smartphones or tablets

carbon footprint
The amount of harmful carbon
dioxide that is released into
the atmosphere as a result of
one person's activities

cyberbullying
Bullying that takes place online
or using internet-based apps

digital
Technology that involves
computers

download
To take information or files from
the internet and store them on
your computer

internet
The vast electronic network that
allows billions of computers
from around the world to connect
to each other

malware
A dangerous computer program
that is created to damage or
disable other digital devices

online
Being connected to the internet
via a computer or digital device

passcode
A password made up of numbers or
letters that prevents access to
your digital device

search engine
A computer program that carries
out a search of available
information on the internet
based on the words you type in

smartphone
A mobile phone that is capable
of connecting to the internet

social media
Websites that allow users to
share content and information
online

trusted adult
An adult you know well and trust
who can help you with all issues
relating to the internet

virtual reality (VR)
Computer generated environment
that people can interact with

website
A collection of web pages that
is stored on a computer and made
available to people over the
internet

HELPFUL WEBSITES

Digital Citizenship

The following websites have helpful information about digital citizenship for young people:

http://www.digizen.org/kids/

http://www.digitalcitizenship.nsw.edu.au/Prim_Splash/

http://www.cyberwise.org/digital-citizenship-games

Bullying

These websites have excellent advice for kids who are experiencing bullying online:

https://www.childline.org.uk/info-advice/bullying-abuse-safety/types-bullying/online-bullying/

http://www.bullying.co.uk

https://www.stopbullying.gov/kids/facts/

Staying Safe

These websites are dedicated to keeping kids safe online, with lots of good advice:

http://www.childnet.com/young-people/primary

http://www.kidsmart.org.uk

http://www.safetynetkids.org.uk/personal-safety/staying-safe-online/

http://www.bbc.co.uk/newsround/13910067

INDEX